Celebrations

EASTER

Hilary Lee-Corbin

Wayland

Celebrations

Christmas
Easter
Hallowe'en
Harvest

New Year
Hindu Festivals
Jewish Festivals
Muslim Festivals

All words that appear in **bold** are
explained in the glossary on page 46

First published in 1989 by
Wayland (Publishers) Limited
61 Western Road, Hove
East Sussex BN3 1JD, England

© Copyright 1989 Wayland (Publishers) Limited

British Library Cataloguing in Publication Data
Lee-Corbin, Hilary
  Easter
  1. Easter
  I. Title II. Series
  394.2'68283

ISBN 1 85210 740 5

Phototypeset by Kalligraphics Limited, Horley, Surrey, England
Printed and bound in Italy by G. Canale & C.S.p.A., Turin

Contents

Celebrating Easter

When we think of Easter we think of fun and games and Easter eggs. It is a very old festival. Long ago it was held to celebrate the coming of spring.

Easter is also the oldest Christian festival. At Easter Christians remember how Jesus died on the cross and how he came back to life again.

So Easter is really two festivals in one. The spring festival is older than the Christian one.

At Easter, Christians have special church services.

Dressing as an Easter bunny is part of the fun of the festival.

The story of Easter

Spring celebrations

Long ago, people thought their gods made the sun die in winter and be born again in spring. All through the cold winter months nothing grew in the fields. Food supplies began to run low. As the winter went on, people did all they could to please the gods.

At last the sun started climbing higher in the sky. New life was starting everywhere. This was the time for everyone to have the biggest celebration of the year.

This ancient spring god was called the Green Man.

Long ago, before Christianity, people believed in many different gods and goddesses. In the lands of the north, people thought the goddess Eostre brought the world to life again in spring. Her name has given us the word 'Easter'.

In old lands of the Middle East, the spring god was called Adonis.

Celebrations long ago

Morris dances were invented before Christianity came to Britain. They are still danced today.

The sun was an important god. In spring, when the day became as long as the night, everyone got up before dawn. They climbed a hill and danced and sang with joy as the sun rose. Winter was over.

8

The Celts were people who lived in Britain long ago. They lit bonfires at dawn to celebrate spring. Then they marched to a magic tree which they decorated with evergreens and flowers. There holy men killed a bull and some lambs. Then the people prayed for good crops and lots of children to be born. Afterwards everyone had a feast. The children gave each other painted eggs. This was to show that new life had come to the earth.

➡

The main Christian festival

When the people in Britain became Christians, they did not stop having an Easter festival. Instead of celebrating the coming of spring, they celebrated Jesus rising from the dead.

At Easter time, fires were lit in churches and candles were burned. In Sweden, girls still wear crowns of candles at Easter time.

In those early years, Easter was held at different times by Christians in different lands. So holy leaders decided that Easter Day should be held on the same day, a Sunday, everywhere in the world.

As years went by, Easter-time celebrations lasted longer. Today, for most people, Easter starts with **Palm Sunday** and ends eight days later with the Easter Monday Bank Holiday. Christians call this **Holy Week**. These girls are part of a Holy Week procession in Brazil, in South America.

11

Holy Week

Palm Sunday

Holy Week starts with Palm Sunday. That is the day when Christians remember the time Jesus rode into Jerusalem on a donkey. Many people called him King and tore branches down from the palm trees and threw them on the ground for him to ride over.

Blessing and giving out palm-leaf crosses is still done in some churches. These children holding palm leaves live in Spain. They are in a Palm Sunday procession. In Britain and other northern lands where palm trees will not grow, evergreen branches are often used instead. They are used to decorate churches.

In Italy, olive branches are used instead of palms. In Jerusalem, people follow the path which Jesus took. In parts of Germany, at one time, priests used to ride to church on a donkey on Palm Sunday. It reminded people of Jesus's journey.

Maundy Thursday

The Bible tells us that on the day before he was killed, Jesus washed the feet of his disciples. This was to show that even the most important people should be humble.

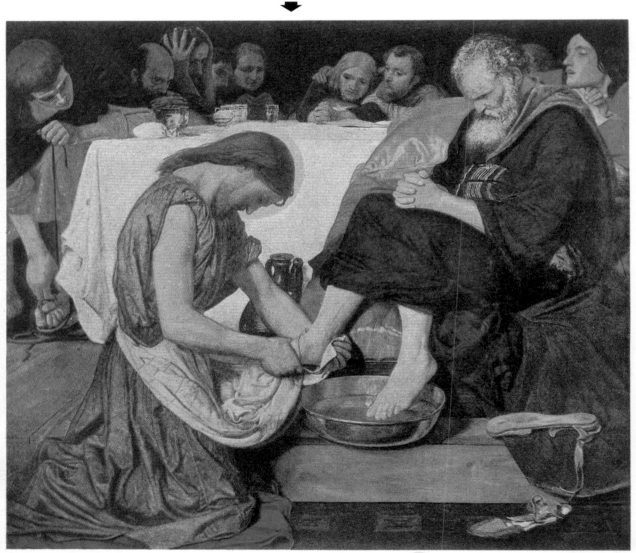

In later years, priests used to wash the feet of poor people to show they had learned the lesson taught by Jesus. Afterwards, they gave out gifts of money or food. As time went by, even kings washed people's feet.

In Rome the Pope washes the feet of priests and then serves them bread and wine.

This idea lives on in **Maundy Thursday** celebrations in Britain. That is the day when the Queen gives special coins called **'Maundy money'** to one old man and one old woman for each year that the Queen has lived.

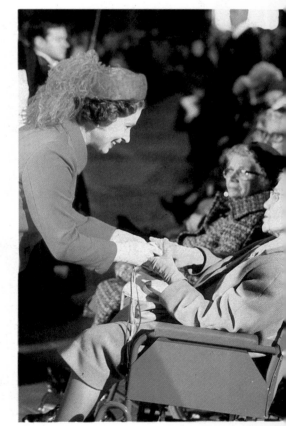

Good Friday

For Christians, **Good Friday** was the day when Jesus was killed. It is a day when many people feel sorry for the wrong things they have done.

Today, it is still a sad day for lots of people. In Mexico, Christians often wear black on Good Friday.

It is thought that the name 'Good Friday' may have started as 'God's Friday'. Over the years the name changed. Or perhaps it comes from the days when 'Good' meant 'Holy'.

Whatever the meaning of its name, Good Friday is thought to be unlucky in all Christian lands.

Years ago, many people would not work on that day because they thought it would bring bad luck. Blacksmiths, who use iron to make horseshoes, did not work on that day because iron nails had been used to fasten Jesus to the cross.

17

Easter Day

Lighting fires, ringing bells, eating chocolate eggs, singing hymns — these are all part of Easter Day celebrations. After the sadness of Good Friday, this is the joyful part of Easter.

Churches that have been kept black and bare are decorated with flowers. For Christians, this is the most holy day of the year. They remember the day when Mary went to the tomb where Jesus was buried. The body was gone. Two angels told Mary that Jesus was alive again.

These Russian people are giving friends Easter eggs on Easter Day, many years ago.

Jesus coming back to life was something wonderful. It showed Christians that Jesus really was the Son of God. It is not surprising that they started celebrating the day that Christ rose from the dead, instead of spring.

Easter Monday

Easter Monday is a day for games and sports, from football to motor racing. One of the oldest games that children play is rolling hard-boiled eggs down hills, to see which will get to the bottom first.

Many kinds of ball games were played. In one English town there were so many games that the day after Easter was called 'Ball Monday'.

Sometimes people did special Easter dances, using Easter eggs.

Motor racing is a popular sport on Easter Bank Holiday. Our Easter holiday ends after the Monday, but years ago nobody worked on the second Monday and Tuesday after Easter either. It was called **'Hocktide'**. These were also days for sport.

Sometimes, on Hocktide Monday, women would take ropes and catch any man they came across. He would be tied up unless he gave them money. The next day it was the men's turn to catch the women. The money was given to the church or to the poor.

Hares, rabbits and eggs

Hares and rabbits

This German Easter card shows rabbits and hares
filling baskets with painted eggs.

In lots of countries, children get up early on Easter Day and go around their houses and gardens looking for Easter eggs.  Maybe you do. Maybe you were told when you were very young that the eggs were hidden by the Easter hare or rabbit. How did this story start?

Long ago, people believed that the Easter hare belonged to the goddess of spring, Eostre. Parents told their children that the magic hare would leave presents for them. These were usually painted hens' eggs. That is why pictures of hares and rabbits are often seen on Easter cards.

The eggs that we get today are usually made of chocolate.

Easter eggs

We see lots of eggs at Easter because they remind us that a new life is just ready to start — the baby chick in the egg!

Long ago, people ate eggs at spring festivals and used egg shapes in their pictures. This was before Jesus Christ was born. Many years after that, Christians took eggs to church at Easter time for blessing.

Painting eggs goes back a long, long time. In China, people used to give each other red or decorated eggs at their spring festival. Cardboard eggs with a decorated shell and a present inside were the next to be made. After that, eggs were made out of marzipan and, later, chocolate.

You can still buy decorated cardboard eggs to put small presents inside.

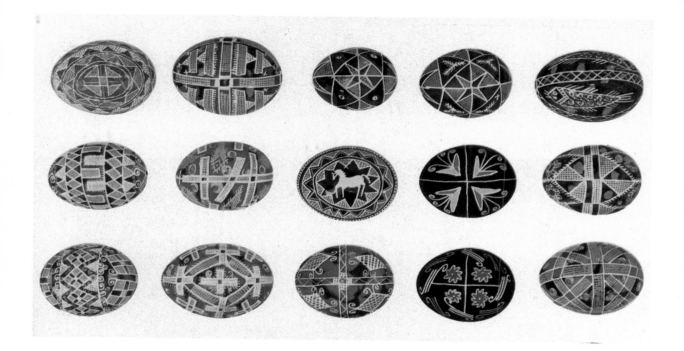

These beautiful painted eggs are from Germany.

Easter eggs can be decorated with any colour. The easiest way is to put some food colouring in the water when you boil the eggs. Or you can try natural dyes. Spinach in the water turns eggs green. Beetroot turns them red. Tea dyes them dark brown. Onion skins make them golden.

You can draw a pattern on your egg with a white wax crayon. Then dip it in the food colouring. The wax keeps the colouring away, so you will get a pattern on your egg where the wax was drawn.

Of course, you can also boil an egg in clear water and then paint it afterwards. That is what these children are doing.

Egg games

Rolling Easter eggs down a slope is a game children have played for many years. This still goes on in the north of England, Scotland, and the USA.

Special Easter games take place at the White House, where the American President lives. Every year, crowds of children are allowed into the gardens of the White House on Easter Monday to roll eggs.

This is a very old Easter egg game.

An egg-rolling game on the lawns of the White House is about to start.

Another egg game is called 'egg-shackling'. This is played like conkers. Each of the two players holds a hard-boiled egg in one hand. Then they bang the eggs together until one breaks.

Egg games began in the old spring festivals. People played them because they thought it would help farmers have a good harvest that year.

Sports and games

Lifting and ducking

Some very strange Easter games used to be played in the past.

'Lifting' was one of these. Chairs were decorated with evergreen branches and carried around the village by young men. Girls had to sit in these chairs and be lifted high into the air. The next day it was the women's turn to lift the men.

Nowadays many people like to go to watch horse-racing on Easter Monday. Or they might watch racing on television.

Long ago, water was part of some old Easter games. In some countries Easter Monday was called 'Ducking Monday'. Young girls were thrown in ponds or lakes. The girls were expected to find this funny. They were told it would make them better wives and more likely to have children!

Hallaton's Easter games

This strange Easter game is called 'bottle kicking'. It is played in England, in a small village called Hallaton. The bottles are really small wooden barrels of beer. Men from Hallaton play against men from other villages. They try to kick the barrels over lines that are drawn a long way apart.

Many sports are played at Easter. One of the most popular ball games in Britain is football.

Another game is played at Hallaton before the bottle kicking begins. This is called 'hare pie scrambling', but there is no hare in the pie!

Instead, a big beef pie is cut up and carried to a place called Hare Pie Bank. The pieces are thrown into a crowd of people, who all try to grab a bit. No-one knows how or when these games started.

Foods and feasting

Food plays an important part in the Easter celebrations.

For lunch on Easter Day, roast lamb is often eaten. In Italy, the lamb is eaten with a special salad made with hard-boiled eggs. In other places veal is enjoyed, as well as big custard tarts.

In Poland, the kitchen table is covered with evergreen leaves and then Easter food is put on it. Before anything can be eaten it must be blessed by a priest. In towns, the priest cannot go to every house, so the children carry some of the food to church to be blessed.

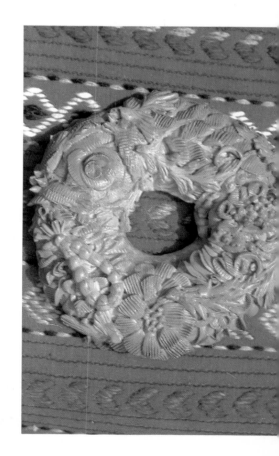

This is a ring of Easter bread from the Greek island of Crete.➤

34

Hot cross buns are eaten on Good Friday. The cross on top reminds people of the cross on which Jesus died on Good Friday.

Parades

In spring, as the weather becomes warmer, people enjoy putting on new clothes. People have always dressed up at Easter and taken part in parades.

Today, Easter bonnet parades are held. Hats are covered with flowers and bows and the person with the best one wins a prize. These funny hats are in a parade in New York, USA.

➡

Big parades are held in Spain. In a town called
Seville, life-size models showing scenes of the Easter
story are carried through the streets. Men like
these, dressed in strange hoods, walk alongside.
This is to show they are sorry for any wrong they
have done.

Afterwards there is a spring fair. For days everyone
dances and sings and enjoys themselves in their
finest clothes.

Fires and fireworks

Long ago, people lit bonfires at Easter to show their gods how happy they were that the cold days of winter were over.

In Sweden and West Germany, people still light bonfires. Some people believe that bonfires and fireworks will frighten away evil spirits.

In other lands they have bonfires on Good Friday. In Portugal, dolls supposed to be Judas are burned in the flames. Judas was the man who gave Jesus away to his enemies. These Portuguese sailors are beating a straw doll that is supposed to be Judas.

A special service is held in some churches on the night before Easter Day. The whole church is kept dark. Then the priest lights one small candle and everyone remembers how Jesus came out of the dark tomb. From this candle, everyone in the church lights a candle of their own. At last the whole church is ablaze with light.

Passion plays

These people are acting in a Good Friday Passion play in Poland.

Long before there were any books, people heard about Jesus by listening to stories. The most important story was the Easter story. To help everyone remember it, it was put into a play called a **'Passion play'**.

Passion plays were acted in all Christian countries. One village in West Germany, called Oberammergau, became specially famous.

Long ago a terrible disease called the Black Death killed many people. Some of the villagers of Oberammergau died from it. When the disease went away the people were so pleased that they promised to act a Passion play every ten years. This was to thank God. To this day they have kept their promise.

This young girl is playing the part of an angel in such a play. ▶

Spring festivals around the world

Japan has a colourful spring festival called the 'Change of Season'. Roast beans are thrown around to drive away evil spirits.

The Hindu spring festival in India is held in February or early March. Fires play a very important part. There are parades and dancing in the streets. Often, people cover each other with coloured powder, or spray each other with coloured water.

The Sikhs in India celebrate with a festival of sports and games. It lasts three days.

People living in the southern half of the world, such as Australia and New Zealand, celebrate Easter at the end of their summer. They have sports and games, and Easter eggs are hidden for children to find, even though it is not springtime.

Easter in the future

Spring festivals were held to celebrate the end of winter. Also, people prayed for new crops of food and for more animals to be born. Today, in places like Britain and North America, people do not have to worry so much about winter cold and whether their crops will grow. So, will the Easter festival fade away? It seems unlikely.

Easter will go on, for two reasons. First, it is the most important time of the year for Christians. It will always be a time for religious celebration. The second reason is that people need holidays. They like to forget work and to enjoy themselves.

44

⬆

Easter parades are enjoyed by people of all ages.
They enjoy having a holiday when spring arrives.

45

Glossary

Good Friday The day when Jesus was put to death on the cross.

Hocktide The second Monday and Tuesday after Easter. These used to be holidays, too.

Holy Week The time from Palm Sunday to Easter Bank Holiday Monday.

Maundy money Money given to old people by the Queen on Maundy Thursday. She gives money to one man and one woman for each year of her life, so when she was 50 she gave Maundy money to 50 men and 50 women.

Maundy Thursday The day when Christians remember the time Jesus washed the feet of his disciples.

Palm Sunday The Sunday before Easter, when Christians remember Jesus riding into Jerusalem on a donkey. Palm leaves were put down for him to ride over.

Passion play A play that acts out the Easter story of Jesus's death and resurrection.

Books to read

If you would like to find out more about Easter, you may like to read the following books:

The Lion Easter Book edited by Mary Batchelor (Lion Publishing, 1987)

Easter Faith by Myrtle Langley (Lion Publishing, 1987)

The First Easter by Catherine Storr (Franklin Watts, 1984)

The Easter Book edited by Felicity Trotman (Hippo Books, 1987)

The Easter Book by Jenny Vaughan (Macdonald, 1986)

Index

Acknowledgements

The publisher would like to thank all those who provided pictures on the following pages: Bruce Coleman Limited 4, 10, 13, 17, 21, 36, 37, 41, 42, 44; Mary Evans Picture Library 12, 14, 18, 22, 24, 26, 30, 38; Outlook Films Ltd. 11; Ann & Bury Peerless 43; PHOTRI 5, 23, 29; Picturepoint Ltd.16, 19, 34, 40, 45; Ronald Sheridan's Photo-Library 6, 7; Syndication International 15; TASS 39; TOPHAM 25; Malcolm S. Walker 27, 32, 35; ZEFA 31, 33.